Sambo- A Mas~~tery Guide to~~ Marti

A Beginner Guide to Sambo Martial Art along with It's Grappling Styles, Throws Holds, and Submission Techniques

Isaac Joy

Contents

INTRODUCTION

SAMozashchita Bez Oruzhiya(SAMBO) (meaning "self-defense without weapons") is a Soviet martial art as well as combat sport. It is a modern form of martial arts that has also been recognized by United World Wrestling as the third style of international wrestling. It is a self-defense martial art that is influenced by Jujutsu, Judo, as well as other forms of martial arts.

In this sport, two people compete against each other while adhering to strict rules and regulations. During the game, the players use various blows and tricks against each other, and they earn points based on their tricks. The match is won by the player with the most points. The players can also win the match by effectively attempting numerous locks or submission trickery on one another and completing the match before the timer runs out.

Before they could even compete in this sport, sambo players have to go through a rigorous training stage.

Players must be able to strike and grapple in the clinch. The match necessitates a high level of aggression while playing. To excel in the match, the players must excel in a variety of skills.

Players has to be agile and flexible, and also learn a variety of throws, joint locks, strikes, kicks, as well as suffocation methods that will be used throughout the game. Since this sport requires excellent control over all skills, having to learn the art takes years of training and dedication.

CHAPTER ONE

Sambo's Brief History

Sambo was created in Russia primarily through the efforts of Vasili Oshchepkov and Viktor Spiridonov. Initially, they formed this art to improve the hand-to-hand combat techniques of the Soviet military. Oschepkov and Spiridinov worked with the Russian government to increase the Red Army's hand-to-hand combat system in 1923.

In 1968, FILA designated sambo as the global level wrestling style. The Federation International Amateur Sambo (FIAS) was founded in 1985 as the first official

Sambo organization, and it was later divided into FIAS East as well as FIAS West.

Sambo was designated as the Soviet Union's official combat sport in 1938. Sambo was a demonstration sport at the 1980 Olympic Games in Moscow, Russia, but it did not make the list due to a boycott.

Countries Taking Part

Sambo, despite being one of the most modern forms of martial arts, is still practiced and played in many countries today due to its universal appeal and unique techniques. Even though it is well-known in Russia, its popularity is gradually spreading throughout the world. Players from various martial arts styles have begun to practice sambo.

Sambo is practiced and played in countries such as Russia, Kazakhstan, Bulgaria, Venezuela, Belarus, Mongolia, Ukraine, Uzbekistan, Serbia, Mongolia, and Japan.

CHAPTER TWO

Overview

SAMBO (unarmed self-defense) (a contraction of the words "self-defense without a weapon") ") - a type of sport fight that originated in the Soviet Union. It is the one who is preoccupied with SAMBO (unarmed self-defense), who physically develops well, has become accustomed to acting in a scenario of single combat, and confiscates the methods that allow it to behave confidently for self-defense. It is difficult to learn "the secrets" of SAMBO (unarmed self-defense).

The technology and tactics of this type of sport are so diverse that it is possible to achieve craftsmanship after only one year of working in a regular occupation.

Enrolling in the section in which the occupations are managed to pass under the supervision of an experienced trainer is the most dependable path to skill of craftsmanship in SAMBO (unarmed self-defense). Such options are beyond exhaustive.

In this case, occupations can be organized independently with the Jacks, military patriotic clubs, schools, and T. p.

The purpose of this article is to provide those who want to be occupied by SAMBO (unarmed self-defense) with basic information on occupation organization.

To organize occupations, do the following:

1. To finish the group. Methods will be improved in a large group setting. It is preferable for there to be an equal number of people in each occupation.

2. To attract experienced athletes or trainers to occupations in the manager's quality. It is possible for management to separate the most physically equipped person, who will perform trainer duties for the first time.

Members of the group must pass a medical examination and obtain a doctor's permission to work in the fight against SAMBO (unarmed self-defense). Please return this information to the trainer.

3. The trainer is ready to conduct occupations. They will initially aid in the suggestion of this guide. Then it is necessary to obtain special educational methods literature,

preferably the book e. [Chumakova] "one hundred lessons of SAMBO (unarmed self-defense) fight." ", the competition rule For each lesson, a summary of occupations that reflects its content should be written ([obshcherazvivayushchie] and special exercises, methods and the forms of struggles).

4. To get the workspace ready for the occupations. During in the winter, occupations were also transferred to lodgings via a fully adapted carpet. Carpet is made of [bortsovskikh] or gymnastic mats covered in cloth or synthetic casing.

If it is not possible to reach mats, carpets can be made from other soft materials such as blankets, carpets, felt, sawdust, straw, and others.

Exercising can be done outside in the summer. For the occupations, they dig a pit 20-30 cm deep and fill it with branches, sawdust, grass, leaves, and T. p. They pack and cover everything with material. The carpet's dimensions are such that each person who occupies it receives at least 4 square meters of space.

5. Melting, cowards, SAMBO (unarmed self-defense) jacket (can be supplemented with a coat) as well as a cloth belt

and boots (which can be replaced with Czech women in the limiting case by clean noses edges).

There must be no metallic or plastic fastenings, buckles, buttons, or other embellishments on footwear or clothing.

6. To create a training schedule. Occupations last 60-90 minutes. During the week, I have 2-3 occupations at the same time.

7. To be affiliated with the SAMBO fight federation (unarmed self-defense). To establish a reputation for occupational organization. To learn about the competition calendar and T. p.

8. So every occupation is divided into three parts: preparatory, fundamental, and final. The preparatory phase includes a comprehensive set of [obshchepodgotovitelnykh] exercises, such as running, leaping, and actions, that allow for maximum amplitude motions in various joints, particularly the humeral, elbow, neck, spine, and feet.

The special exercises of [samostrakhovki], as well as the motions that help later to study methods, are performed in the second half of the preparatory part. as well as to carry out training struggles The methods of struggle are studied and improved in the majority of the occupation (in the fight). Those who are occupying are dispersed to the vapors for this purpose. In the vapors, partners are chosen based on their weight and growth. During the course of a study, one person employs a method, while another aids it.

The partner must not resist in this case. Since one champion will master the method, those who are occupied will switch roles. Both champions closely monitor the correctness of motion execution (method or [samostrakhovki]) and correct each other's errors.

Following the study of methods, the champions engage in battles in which they attempt to carry out methods on the opposing partner. It is necessary to strictly adhere to the competition rules during the struggles.

During occupations (struggles), it is prohibited to: throw with confiscation for the head, throw with confiscation to the painful methods, fall on the enemy by entire body, make strangling seizures, press mouth, nose, deliver impacts, scratch, bite, make painful methods to the spine, to be abutted against the person, to seize fingers, to carry out excruciating methods in the counter, to seize after cowards, to seize from within the sleeves.

The exercises that allow all systems of the organism of those occupying to be put into a state of rest are given at the end.

The totals of occupations are totaled, and declarations are made. It is necessary to wash out after occupations with a warm shower (in the bath). You will be introduced to the course content in the sections below.

They do not include the [obshcherazvivayushchie] exercises that are given in each lesson to develop qualities such as quickness, force, adroitness, flexibility, equilibrium, and others. The given lessons - this is only a diagram that must be followed, supplemented with its various exercises for overall development. The amount of exercise prescribed varies according to physical development, the readiness of those occupying, and the trainer.

CHAPTER THREE

Lessons 1-5 of SAMBO (Unarmed Self-Defense).

1st occupation

• Combat training.

• Run.

• [Obshcherazvivayushchie] flexibility exercises

• [Samostrakhovka] with a sideways drop (Fig. 1). Those in the study end position drop, then return to this position by moving backwards from the sitting position (complete [priseda], crouch, counter).

Рис. 1

• Thrust from the rear step (Fig. 2). The champion employs another technique of [samostrakhovki] from the thrust by dropping on the side.

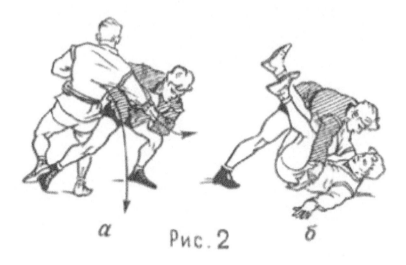

a Рис. 2 *б*

• Retention on both sides (Fig. 3). One champion enables the partner to retain himself, and then he starts to be freed, being relocated with minimal force, so that the partner can understand to retain the resisting partner. Once it realizes to retain, it can leave with full force.

Finally, it is possible to engage in combat. One champion is on the spin, unable to be turned for the stomach and unable to allow another one to take himself for retention. Seconds through 30-40 champions switch roles, then the champion seizes partner, who is located on the other side.

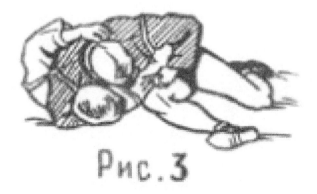

Рис. 3

Occupation 2

• Following the [obshcherazvivayushchikh] limbering-up exercises, the champions begin studying [samostrakhovki] with the drop on the back.

Рис.4

The end position (Fig. 4) is researched first, followed by a drop by returning to the sitting position ([priseda], crouch, costing) with the fixation of the end position. Repeat the drop on the side from the first lesson, but this time add passage into the end position by having to move from one side to the other and the drop through the stick back (Fig. 5).

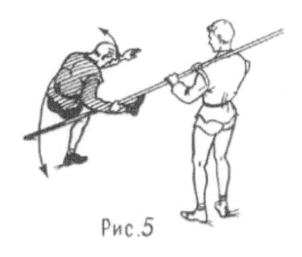

Рис.5

• Investigation of thrust by lateral hewing (Fig. 6). When the partner costs but does not move his or her foot, the thrust is studied by the hewing. When the partner moves, the thrust is studied by the hewing (stepping back, it moves to the side).

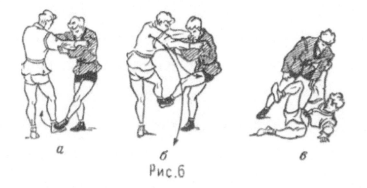

а   б   в

Рис.6

• Revolutionary hand seizure from the side (Fig. 7). Overturning to the back of a partner who is on all fours. To carry out retention on the side after the revolution. The first partner doesn't really object. After mastering [sambistom] of the revolution method, the partner could perhaps resist after seizure, and then it can resist and refuse to give its hand.

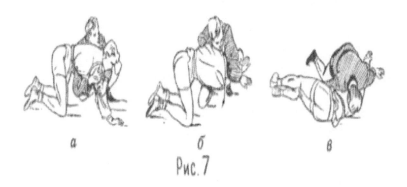

a   б   в

Рис. 7

Occupation 3

• Research the techniques of [samostrakhovki] with drop forward and hand support. First, exercises from of the original position of support lying are performed - flexure and straightening of the hands. Then, from the same starting position, cotton is carried out by the palms well before breast, being repulsed, and returning after cotton into the support lying.

16

Hands amortize, being bent, from the initial position being worthwhile only on elbows of hand is for back to fall forward on hands, without regard for the carpet's breast (Fig. 8). The exercise in position costing must be repeated.

a   Рис.8   *б*

• Hook thrust from within (Fig. 9). Partner costs, with widely spaced feet To hook from within its foot as well as stretch to itself, pushing downward from within itself.

Рис.9

• Painful method involving the use of an elbow lever through the thigh (Fig. 10). Following the completion of the retention on the side, the method is carried out.

To take the attacked's forearm and finish harvesting to the thigh of the foot that is lying on the carpet, so that the arm will indeed lie down on the thigh and the forearm would descend to the carpet between the feet.

At the present time of total straightening of the hand, the partner should say "to eat" or slap with the free hand all through the body of that able to conduct method or along the carpet. The conducting technique is terminated on this signal. The battle begins after both champions have completed their methods. One champion takes another for retention, and he tries to carry out a painful method, which is opposed by another. The champions' roles shift between the ages of 20 and 30.

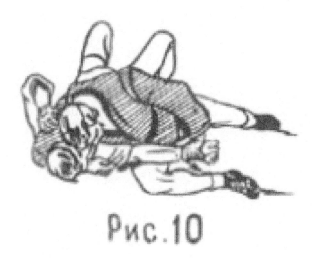

Рис.10

Occupation 4

• The somersaults forward (Fig. 11) and the drop thru the stick forward are included in the preparatory part, along with other workouts and previously studied techniques of [samostrakhovki] (Fig. 12).

Рис. 11

Рис. 12

• Front step thrust (Fig. 13). To turn his back to his partner, to place his foot so that his thigh rests on his foot higher than his elbow, and to throw forward before itself. That falling gets to carry out [samostrakhovku] in the side drop.

Рис. 13

• Retention across (Fig. 14). Beds on top, across to the enemy's breast, to keep his hands or hand and leg.

Рис.14

• Fight for retention across the board. Following a seizure, the stomach is attempted to overturn. Then the situation becomes complicated: one is lying on the spin, and another is attempting to take it for retention.

• Struggle with the lying position. Both champions lie down on their backs and attempt to overturn and take mate for the retention on the signal. It conquers the one whom it had previously taken as an enemy for the sake of retention.

Occupation 5

• [Samostrakhovka] with drop from the thrust thru the head (Fig. 15). Beginning with [kuvyrok], the champion caves in after coming into contact with the carpet blades and moves into the position depicted in the figure.

Рис.15

•Striving for the crown (Fig. 16). Sitting closer to the partner's legs and also being abutted by foot against the stomach to keep moving the enemy across itself.

Partner performs previously studied [samostrakhovku].

Рис.16

• After side retention, use a lever of the elbow thru the forearm for a painful method (Fig. 17). Following retention just on side, this same champion releases the partner's head but rather seizes his arm, then seizes the partner's forearm and unbends it.

Рис. 17

• The struggle begins after the technique has been studied. One of the retention stances must employ a painful method, which another opposes. They then switch places.

CHAPTER FOUR

Lessons 6-10 of SAMBO (Unarmed Self-Defense).

Occupation 6

• [Samostrakhovka] with the backward drop, turning, as well as hand support (Fig. 18). After costing the champion, it falls back from the position, and in the drop, it is turned with assist to the hands (see occupation 3). Turning is done as little angle to a carpet as possible.

Рис .18

The study of thrust by destabilization by the push (Fig. 19). This type of attack draws the opponent to itself and tries to pull it downward. Then, by pushing the adversary downward and attempting to attack, he is thrown to the back. Partner does [samostrakhovku] with drop on the back by moving.

Рис.19

• Research on the lever revolution (Fig. 20). The partner stands with all fours after lowering his head and arranging his hands. To keep moving to the enemy's side, face his head, put one hand on his neck, as well as take this hand from within with the other hand. That offensive draws the enemy's hands upward – to itself, and also the enemy's head inclines straight down and, beds by the breast forward to enemy's hand, turns him over to back.

Рис.20

• Using the methodological approach, the champions should try to overthrow each other while resisting seizure. Only one way to generate resistance is to tense your muscles.

• Perform a struggle in the fight while lying at the end of the lesson. All revolutions, retention, as well as painful methods that have been studied can be used.

Occupation 7

• Repeat [samostrakhovki] with drop back on the partner's back (see occupation 4).

• Foot seizure-induced thrust (Fig. 21).

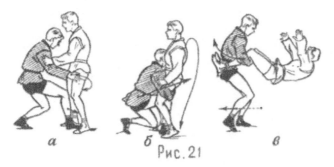

а   б   в
Рис. 21

The champion grabs his partner's legs and lifts them upward. Retreats with partners, able to perform [samostrakhovku] as previously learned.

• Withdrawal from the sitting side of retention (Fig. 22).

Рис. 22

Partner retains on the side, [vynosya] both feet forward in front of the enemy's head. Raising one's feet and then sharply lowering them to sit, after overturning it to the back.

• Fights for the implementation of methodologies in the fight against deception.

Occupation 8

• In limbering-up to include bridge exercises. They prepare to [samostrakhovke] with the drop on the head for protection from retention and painful methods. To lie back on the carpet, then cave in and rise to the bridge, with concern for the carpet's forehead and the possibility of the chin. To repeat this motion 8-10 times. Then, after turning the head (first to one side, then to the other), repeat the

Рис. 23

• Belt seizure with a thrust through the thigh (Fig. 24).

Рис. 24

Being turned away from the partner, by basin to line its feet back - upward and to throw ahead of itself. Partner performs [samostrakhovku] by dropping on the side.

• Painful method - unit across (Fig. 25).

Рис. 25

After retaining across the attacking hand, it seizes the forearm of the distant hand of the enemy in the wrist, superimposes a brush on top and forces the seized forearm against the carpet, some other hand it brings underneath the arm of partner, seizes the forearm on top by its hand. The painful method of signaling about the delivery is carried out by revolving the arm of the seized hand of the enemy. When partner resists conducting method after seizure, one should attempt to make the method after fulfillment.

• Struggle in the fight for the fulfillment of the researched methods.

Occupation 9

• To perform the exercise "getting up to the bridge from the position costing." This exercise allows you to create [samostrakhovki] habits with a drop on the head (Fig. 26[a]).

a   Рис.26   б

The first exercise is performed with the assistance of a partner. If the champion has good flexibility and descends smoothly to the bridge, it is possible to try to reach the bridge without the assistance of a partner (Fig. 26 [b]).

• Internal revolution with the seizure of an arm and a leg (Fig. 27).

a   Рис.27   б

• • Struggles in the counter (one champion attacks, another defends), champions switch roles after 2-3 minutes.

• Has difficulty fighting lying. Any of the investigated methods can be carried out in 2-3 minutes.

Occupation 10

• Repetition of [samostrakhovki] studied methods (drop on the side from a height of 20-30 cm, from the bench, chair). The same goes for the back.

• Pickup thrust (Fig. 28).

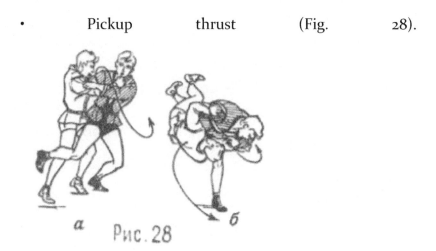

Рис. 28

Turning back to the partner and lining up his distant foot from the front.

• Withdrawal from the retention on the side, twisting out (Fig. 29).

Рис.29

To release the seized hand with a jerk to itself and to overturn to the stomach while being turned by the breast to the partner.

• Attempts to withdraw from the retention on the side.

• Counter squabbles and deception (it is possible to carry out all methods).

CHAPTER FIVE

Lessons 11-15 of SAMBO (Unarmed Self-Defense).

Occupation 11

• Getting ready to repeat [samostrakhovku] from occupation 4. (Fig. 12).

Рис. 12

hen, to complicate its execution, being situated first in 2-3 steps from the stick, approaching it in rapid steps and having to carry out seizure, to make [kuvyrok] through it without a halt. It is possible to complicate the execution of this method even further by approaching a stick by run.

• Front hewing thrust (Fig. 30).

a Рис.30 *б*

Lining a partner's opposite leg into a forward section of the shin, then jerking the hands forward to force it forward. Place [Samostrakhovka] to one side.

• Struggles to see hewings through. Partners' task is to "catch the moment," line the foot, and execute the thrust without expending too much force.

• Withdrawal from the side retention, wringing out the head with hand and leg (Fig. 31).

Рис.31

Champion wrings out partner's head first with his hands (hand), then with his foot as well as overturns partner to its feet.

• Fight struggles relating to retention just on side and withdrawals from it.

• The battles in which all previously studied methods are permitted to be used.

Occupation 12

• [samostrakhovku] is included in limbering-up with the drop thru the post back on the back (Fig. 32).

Рис. 32

Two occupying hold posts for the ends at elbow level. That having to carry out exercise, falling back, sits down on the carpet through the post, and is then rolled to the back.

- Institutional hook thrust from within (Fig. 33).

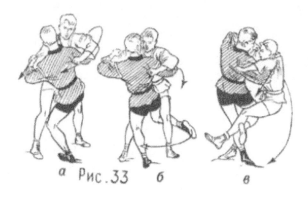

а Рис.33 б в

Without allowing the enemy to spring up by foot to the carpet, to line by its, after catching shin from within, at the moment of the institution (action, as a result of which the enemy makes step for that attacking). To make a jerk with both hands, transferring the weight of the enemy's body to the hooked foot.

- Thrust - heaping up by [zashagivaniem] (Fig. 34).

Рис.34

The conducting method is in the counter, while the partner stands on a elbow (elbows). to sharply extend partner to itself - downward and overturn to the back while simultaneously stepping over through it

• Fight - the champions' initial position, one on the elbows, the other in the counter. The task is to create retention.

• Struggle - one attacks, another defends. After 4-5 minutes, the champions switch roles.

Occupation 13

• The exercise of [samostrakhovki] with drop back on the forearms is included in limbering-up (Fig. 35).

Рис.35

That occupying begins to slant back, then turns 180° and falls just on stomach, backed by the coupled hands.

• Pickup thrust (Fig. 36).

Рис.36

That conducting turns around with its back to the partner and then lines the enemy's legs from the front, whereas the partner falls sideways and carries out [samostrakhovku].

- From the side, head retention (Fig. 37).

Рис.37

Enemy is spinning, attacking from the side of the head on the elbows, of been forced by breast against enemy's breast, and after divorcing widely to the sides of the foot, attacking seizes that attacked's belt.

Occupation 14

• Include [samostrakhovki] workouts with the drop to the side as well as hand support in your limbering-up routine (Fig. 38).

Рис. 38

• Shin-to-shin thrust into the stomach through the head (Fig. 39).

α   Рис. 39   δ

During the spin, the champion seizes the enemy's belt with a similar arm, one foot is placed between both the enemy's legs, another one is abutted by shin against stomach – it tends to fall on the back, having to carry along out for itself, and it moves through itself with the push of foot.

- Impingement of the Achilles tendon (Fig. 40)

Рис.40

- the agonizing method of capturing an opponent's leg under the arm by pressing on the Achilles tendon with radius. The assaulting head of the radius shifts Achilles tendon towards to the side and presses under it by unbending the enemy's seized leg's foot as well as forcing it against its side.

• Problems with the parquet.

Occupation 15

• [Samostrakhovka] with a sideways drop back through the partner Occupation 15 (Fig. 41).

Рис. 41

Internal heel seizure thrust (Fig. 42).

Рис. 42

• Withdrawal from the retention across the neck caused by a seizure and supported by the forearm into the stomach (Fig. 43).

Рис.43

• Partners' resistance to change.

CHAPTER SIX

Lessons 16-20 of SAMBO (Unarmed Self-Defense)

Occupation 16

• [Samostrakhovka] with drop sideways forward through partner Occupation 16 (Fig. 44).

Рис.44

• Foot seizure thrusts their [vynosya] to the side (Fig. 45).

Рис.45

• Withdrawal from of the retention on the other side of the bridge, with the enemy hauled through itself (Fig. 46).

Рис.46

• The difficulties (partners change counter).

Occupation 17

• [Samostrakhovka] with the drop on the breast from of the leap Occupation 17 (Fig. 47).

Рис. 47

• A thrust through the thigh, followed by a seizure of the partner's belt through the same arm (Fig. 48).

Рис. 48

• On 2 minutes, struggles with belt seizure through the opposite arm.

• Excruciating method involving the seizure of the hand between the legs (Fig. 49).

Рис.49

That attack presses and unbends the partner's hand with its legs.

• Struggle - the attacking hand presses the coupled hands of the partner, then attempts to straighten the hand, but the partner resists.

• Struggle for 6 minutes.

Occupation 18

• [Samostrakhovka] with the drop sideways by leaping forward - upward with the assistance of a partner for the hand (Fig. 50).

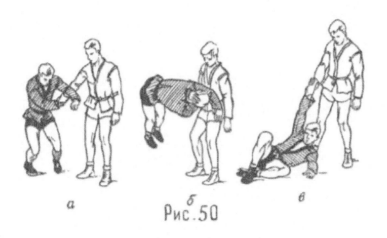

a   б   в

Рис.50

Study of a preparatory exercise for the thrust by sagging -
"thrust by effigy sagging" (Fig. 51).

Рис. 51

Falling back, straightening legs, forming a stomach effigy,
and performing a hand jerk upward - for itself. A bag, a
ball, or other objects can be used in place of the effigy.

47

- Slanting   seizure   revolution   (Fig.   52).

Рис.52

That attacking superimposes the forearm of the distant hand on the neck of the partner on all fours, carries out another hand under the arm and the breast, and connects hands. • Struggles at the fight lying to the revolutions, retention, and painful methods, pressing on the neck on top as well as pushing by arm body, is turned over mate to the back.

Occupation 19

• [Samostrakhovka] with the somersault in air drop on the back (Fig. 53).

Рис.53

• Front step thrust with arm and leg seizure (Fig. 54).

Рис.54

49

• Retention even by top with hand seizure (Fig. 55).

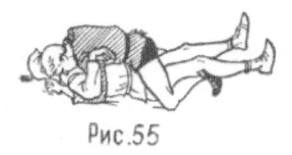

Рис.55

• In the struggle against thrusts with the feet. At the fight, there is a struggle for retention and withdrawal from them.

Occupation 20

• [Samostrakhovka] with drop by somersault forward through sideways arm (Fig. 56).

a   *б* Рис.56 *в*   *г*

Costing should be done on the elbow first, then from the position costing, and finally from the motion costing (by step, by run).

• Hewing in the front with the drop (Fig. 57).

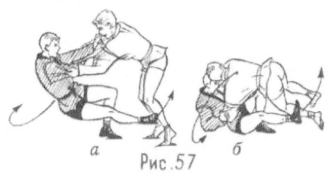

a Рис.57 *б*

Carried along by its partner to hew into the lift of the sole or the lower part of the shin, attempting to toss it upward or interfering with the advancing forward foot.

• From the lower (bed to the back) position, use the elbow as a lever through the forearm (Fig. 58).

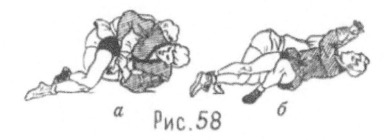

a Рис.58 *б*

• Positional difficulties - one on all fours, another on top

• Counter and lying difficulties

CHAPTER SEVEN

Lessons 21-25 of SAMBO (Unarmed Self-Defense)

Occupation 21

• Repetition - effigy thrust by sagging in the drop

• Outside, revolution with the seizure of an arm and a leg (the enemy stands on all fours) (Fig. 59).

Рис.59

• Thrust by lateral hewing with feet crossed (Fig. 60).

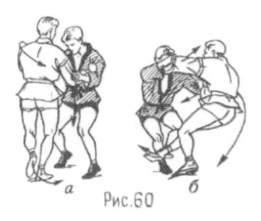

Рис.60

Lateral hewing must be performed while the enemy's leg is not loaded. For example, while moving to the right, the enemy crosses his feet, putting the leftist from behind to the right.

When it begins to rise from the carpet with its right foot in order to transfer it to the right and create a more stable position, it must quickly hew with its left foot.

If the enemy in the right counter moves all around champion to the left from it without crossing his feet, then at the moment of setting its right leg to the carpet, it follows with a jerk of hands to transfer the weight of the enemy and to steeply stretch by left hand to him- and a little downward, but right - from himself and a little upward. This enemy's body will be turned to the left, and the left foot will begin to cross after the right. To get out of this precarious position, the enemy will shift his weight to his left foot and try to set aside to the right. When it raises the right foot, it must be hewn immediately.

• Struggles with change in the hewings' partners.

Occupation 22

• [Kuvyrok] leaps from his chair.

• Thrust by pickup from within (Fig. 61).

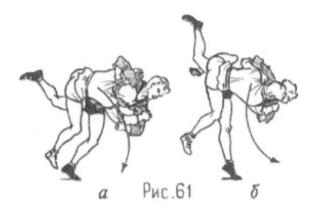

a   Рис.61   б

At the moment of spin reversal, the partner's supporting foot must be placed between his feet.

• Side retention with hand seizure (Fig. 62).

Рис. 62

• Has difficulty with one-sided resistance to foot thrusts. At the trainer's signal, the champions switch roles.

• Individual technological advancement struggles.

Occupation 23

• "Flight -[kuvyrok]" through the lying mat, partner, or chair.

• Thrust through the head with belt seizure through the similar arm and shin support into the stomach (Fig. 63).

Рис.63

• Painful method "opposite unit" across (Fig. 64).

Рис.64

• Struggles in the counter with passage into the fight lying, in order to carry out painful methods

Occupation 24

• [Kuvyrok] returning from the elevation (chair).

• Head thrust with seizure of the neck on top as well as the bodies from below (Fig. 65).

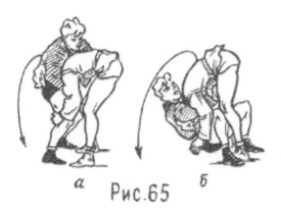

a Рис.65 *б*

In the low counter, the opponent's feet are held together by straight lines. To grab the enemy's neck with one hand and the body with the other (under the stomach).

Hanging on the enemy's neck, settling deeper among his feet and moving across itself.

• Unit-by-foot measurement (Fig. 66).

Рис.66

• 2 X 2 minute struggles with one-sided resistance just at counter and lying

• Struggle.

Occupation 25

• [Kuvyrok] moves forward with the object from the takeoff (weight, ball).

• Take a front step from the elbow (Fig. 67).

a Рис.67   *б*   *в*

Being turned by the partner's back, to get on the side on knee, carrying the enemy forward - to the side.

• Withdraw from the retention across, removing partner's hand as well as head from beneath his or her body (Fig. 68).

Рис. 68

• The unwillingness of partners to change.

CHAPTER EIGHT

Lessons 26-30 of SAMBO (Unarmed Self-Defense).

Occupation 26

• Repeat [samostrakhovki] with the drop forward on the side and partner support for the hand.

• A thrust through the back, followed by the seizure of a hand through the arm (Fig. 69).

Рис.69

Following a turn to move the partner across itself.

• Side retention without seizure of the hand under the arm (Fig. 70).

Рис.70

Sitting on the side, the conducting method seizes the enemy's neck with the neighbor's hand, the jacket in the arm of the neighbor's hand, and forces its head against his head with the other hand.

• Struggles with one-sided resistance in a counter of two 3 minute struggles.

• Has difficulty fighting lying.

Occupation 27

• Exercise repetition - thrust by sagging effigy or bag

• Thrust by [obvivom], seated (Fig. 71).

Рис.71

• Excruciating method - unit by foot from below (Fig. 72).

Рис. 72

• Counter-command struggles - 2 men. X 2 (loss - contact of carpet by anything, besides the soles of feet). One can be attacked by two.

• Efforts to keep the parquet in place.

Occupation 28

• Exercise: two somersaults in a row while lying down (to the side).

• Sagging thrust (Fig. 73).

Рис. 73

To take a partner for the hand and body, to force against itself, and then to fall back and cave in, throwing him through its breast and arm to the carpet.

• Outside, there is a retention across with the seizure of a distant similar hand (Fig. 74).

Рис. 74

• Struggles with one-sided retention resistance.

• Struggles in the counter.

Occupation 29

• [Samostrakhovka] on the back by leaping from a small height (ball, bag, chair).

• Lateral hewing into partner's step rate (Fig. 75).

Рис. 75

To perform by jerking the hands upward - to the side, while simultaneously lining the enemy's leg on the side - outside - from below - upward, with the enemy transferring the weight of the body to this leg after variance to the opposite side. To carry out the enemy's thrust ahead of itself to the back. It must have already been hit at the time of weight transfer to the attacked foot.

• Painful method - lever of elbow, pressing foot by thighs after side retention (Fig. 76).

Рис.76

• Struggles with one-sided opposition in order to fulfill hewings.

• Struggles in accordance with the rules 6 minutes

Occupation 30

• Equilibrium-building exercises (on the spot with the closed eyes and with the rotation by head). To perform 25 nonstop somersaults around the perimeter of the carpet - and then instantly cease costing at the location.

• Thrust - hook from the inside for the same foot (Fig. 77).

Рис. 77

• Excruciating method - elbow lever with seizure of hand between the legs (Fig. 78).

Рис.78

Adversary lies on the spin or on the side; assaulting on the side after taking the rectified neighbor hand with two hands. To stretch the enemy's hand upward - to itself - and to stop the arm by the thighs.

Sitting down, transfer one foot through the neck, then [naklonyas] to the side of the enemy's head, transfer another foot through the body, and bind them.

The enemy's hand is solidly stopped up in between legs, as well as the elbow of the captured hand - is abutted against the attacking hand's stomach. To slowly straighten the enemy's hand to the signal, press the forearm of the seized hand even by forearms of its arms to the breast and cave in.

• Struggles with the thrust's one-sided resistance.

• Struggles in the fight against lying for the purpose of carrying out painful methods.

• Struggles.

CHAPTER NINE

Lessons 31-35 of SAMBO (unarmed self-defense)

Occupation 31

• Repetition of [samostrakhovki] methods.

• Foot seizure with thrust [otkhvatom] (Fig. 79).

Рис.79

• Retention from the side of the head with seizure of the hand (Fig. 80).

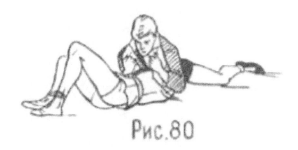

Рис.80

• Fights in the counter-thrust to the clean thrust (which will conquer, who will carry out thrust "purely").

• Fight struggles involving painful methods and protection from them, resulting in a counter.

Occupation 32

• Rep [samostrakhovki] with a drop from the thrust through the head. [Kuvyrok] move forward.

• Thrust through the head with hand seizure and shin support into the thigh (Fig. 81).

a Рис.81 *б*

• Elbow lever seizure with forearm seizure under the arm after top retention (Fig. 82).

Рис.82

• Has problems with closed (tied) eyes.

• Struggles.

Occupation 33

• [Samostrakhovka] - lowering of the foot (jumping off from the height to the stops, to the elbows).

• Internal thrust by [podsadom] (Fig. 83).

Рис.83

• [Spo]c[osoby] of separated coupled hands for performing the painful method by the lever of elbow with confiscation of the hand between legs (Fig. 84)

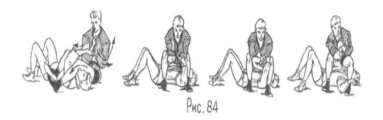

Рис. 84

• One-sided resistance attempts to break the coupled hands (after 2-3 min partners they change by roles).

• Grapples at the counter, in a neighbor's seizure, or in a nearby seizure

Occupation 34

• [Samostrakhovka] - somersaults backwards with the object (effigy, ball and other).

• Internal thrust with arm and leg seizures (Fig. 85).

Рис.85

- Foot retention from the side (Fig. 86).

Рис.86

• Struggles in dealing with one-sided opposition (after 2-3 min partners they change by roles).

• Struggles in the fight stem from changes in the partners (2X3).

Occupation 35

• [Samostrakhovka] - drop forward on side through the partner.

• Thrust by hand seizure under the arm (Fig. 87).

а   Рис.87   б

• Disconnection of the coupled hands, bringing one hand under the forearm and superimposing the other on top (Fig. 88).

Рис.88

CHAPTER TEN

Lessons 36-40 of SAMBO (Unarmed Self-Defense).

Occupation 36

• Equilibrium exercises (on the lath of gymnastic bench). Motions all along line - imitating SAMBO's fighting methods (unarmed self-defense).

• Outside hook thrust -from behind for the distant similar foot (Fig. 89).

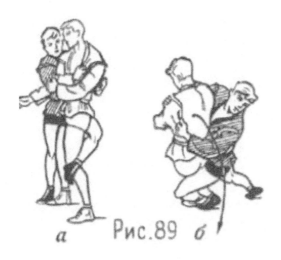

a　Рис.89 *б*

• Detachment of the coupled hands, with the leg abutting the arm of the distant hand (Fig. 90).

Рис.90

Occupation 37

• Exercises with a partner - squatting, inclinations, turnings on the arms with a partner.

• Thrust "by mill" (Fig. 91).

Рис.91

• Withdrawal from the side of the head retention, revolving in the side with the partner (Fig. 92).

Рис.92

• 8-minute struggle at the counter

• Struggle in the fight against withdrawals from retention.

Occupation 38

• Game "eject from the circle" Occupation 38"

• Hook thrust by foot (Fig. 93).

a Рис.93 б в

• Excruciating method - lever to both thighs with shin seizure under arm, being abutted by foot against by the popliteal bend (Fig. 94).

Рис.94

Being abutted from within by a hand against an elbow and straightening its leg, assaulting separates the thighs of the enemy until the signal is given.

• Fights the seizure with one hand.

• Struggles with the odds (strong champion loses 4 marks), struggles last 1-2 minutes.

Occupation 39

• The game is called "cockfighting" (jumping on one foot, by the push of body to force enemy to touch carpet by two feet).

• Outside hook thrust (Fig. 95).

Рис.95

• Retention from the side of the head with reversal of hands and belt (Fig. 96).

Рис.96

Occupation 40

• Jumping from a height to one foot, occupation 40 • Hooks from within with foot seizure • Jump into the height on one foot (Fig. 97).

Рис.97

• Withdrawal from the side of the head retention, wringing out the head, and being turned over to stomach (Fig. 98).

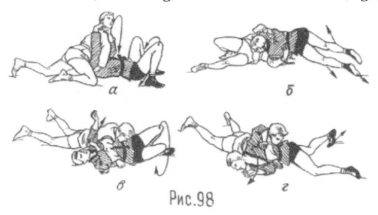

а

б

в

г

Рис.98

• Competitions within the group for withdrawal from retention (it is calculated the number of executed by champion retention and withdrawals from them from the standard position). The twenty-first century was a time of struggle.

CHAPTER ELEVEN

Lessons 41-45 of SAMBO (unarmed self-defense).

Occupation 41

• Champion limbering-up on one's own.

• Thrust through the head, in the side, with the support into the thigh bend (Fig. 99).

a Рис. 99 *б*

- Excruciating method - unit by foot (Fig. 100).

Рис.100

That attacking uses the method of retention on the side with seizure of the neck; the enemy, liberating from the seizure hand, derives it to that attacking's feet and to his head.

The conducting method seizes the wrist of the opposing hand's opposite hand with the free hand, wrings out his hand from its body, and superimposes the humeral part of the hand to its neighbor's thigh. While continuing to wring out the enemy's forearm downward, the shin of the neighbor's foot is superimposed on it, causing the forearm to be located in the popliteal bend.

Moving the heel of one leg with the hooked hand under the other leg, assaulting, raising basin, twisting out the enemy's hand in the humeral joint.

• 2 x 2 minute struggles at the fight lying: competing struggles for group superiority.

Occupation 42

• Destabilization game (to force enemy to touch carpet by anything, besides soles).

• Thrust caused by jerk destabilization with hand and neck seizure (Fig. 101).

a   Рис.101^{б}

• Achilles tendon impingement while lying on the enemy, with seizure of the opposite shin (Fig. 102).

Рис. 102

• Struggles with one-sided resistance to Achilles tendon jamming.

• Struggles to maintain endurance for 20 minutes.

Occupation 43

• Lateral revolution thrust (Fig. 103).

Рис. 103

• Withdrawal as well as protection from retention on the foot's side (Fig. 104).

Рис. 104

• Techniques are combined. Following the seizure of the hand between the legs by the top passage to the elbow lever.

• Handle the partners' aversion to change.

Occupation 44

• Limbering up with somersaults, [samostrakhovki], and T. p.

• Lateral thigh thrust (Fig. 105).

Рис. 105

• Retention at the top via the hook of the feet (Fig. 106).

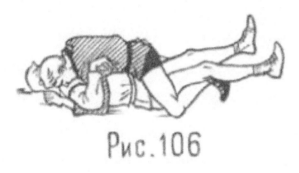

Рис.106

• Combination - top retention, passage to the painful method the arm unit (across).

• Struggles in accordance with competition rules.

Occupation 45

• Exercising to learn about the thrust through the breast (by sagging).

• A thrust through the breast is followed by a seizure of a similar hand as well as body from the side (Fig. 107).

Рис.107

• Achilles tendon impingement caused by seizure of the opposing foot and support underneath the knee of the enemy's other leg (Fig. 94).

Рис.94

CHAPTER TWELVE

Lessons 46-50 of SAMBO (Unarmed Self-Defense).

Occupation 46

• Rear step with hand seizure by two hands and drop (Fig. 108).

Рис. 108

• Retention from the lying side (Fig. 109).

Рис. 109

• Combination - rear step thrusts with drop and retention on the side lying.

• Struggles with the drop thrusts.

Occupation 47

• The thrusts are coupled - hewing is lateral, and the front step is forward.

• Difficult method - use an inside lever (Fig. 110).

Рис. 110

• Struggles.

Occupation 48

• Limbering-up with the beginning of somersaults forward - in side

• After winding with confiscation from the side the similar hand as well as the belt (Fig. 111).

Рис.111

• Apply a lever to both thighs, securing the foot on the arm (Fig. 112).

Рис.112

• Having difficulty at the counter and lying.

Occupation 49

• Exercises for the "scissors" thrust Leap to the partner, one foot to the partner's breast, the other to the thigh.

• "Scissors" thrust (Fig. 113).

Рис.113

• Elbow lever with foot clamped by thighs (Fig. 114).

Рис.114

• Struggles.

Occupation 50

• Applying "Scissors" to one foot (Fig. 115),

Рис.115

• Unit by foot measurement (Fig. 116).

Рис.116

• Struggles.

CHAPTER THIRTEEN

SAMBO's classic (Unarmed Self-Defense)

The fight method of SAMBO (unarmed self-defense) is sub - divided in to the fight method costing, fight technique lying, passages from of the fight costing to the fight lying, and passages from the fight lying to the fight costing, according to classification a.A.[Kharlampieva].

Technology fight costing

- Counters, distance, seizure preparation, seizures, movement, and fraudulent motion are all introduced into fight costing technology. Methods for preparing for thrusts, starting positions for conducting thrusts, and approaches [k] to thrusts

- Defensive seizures make a breakthrough.

- Insurance as well as [samostrakhovka].

- Broschi's

- Combinations based on thrusts

- Defends against thrusts.

- Thrusts in both directions.

Distances

SAMBO (unarmed self-defense) distinguishes five distances:

1. Distance from the seizure - [sambisty] they do not concern each other and they explore advantageous for the attack moment, of been moved on the carpet and trying to make all possible dishonest the motion without the seizures enemy.

2. From afar, the champions seize each other's sleeves, one or both by hand.

3. Average distance - [sambisty] they seize each other for clothing on the body from the front and the with one hand for the sleeve, A another - after clothing on the body from front.

4. Neighbor distance - the champions seize with one hand for the sleeve or clothing on the breast, and the other for the clothing on the spin, the winch, or the foot.

5. Close distance - [sambisty] they clench one another, being pushed by the body one to the other or winding foot by foot.

Seizures

Seizures are classified as basic, reciprocal, preliminary, or defensive.

- They are called such seizures because they are carried out for that purpose, in order to carry out thrusts, based on the seizures with the fight costing. It [sambist] achieves them until the moment when the enemy imposes its seizure.

- Reciprocal seizures with fight costing - these such seizures, which it [sambist] carries out in response to enemy seizures, on the basis of conditions given by them. [S] reciprocal by the seizures, they can also be carried out thrusts.

- Seizures are called defensive by the fight costing they are conducted for that, in order to hinder or make impossible the conducting by the enemy of that or another thrust. However, when the seizure is determined to be defensive, it can be used [sambistom] for conducting thrusts.

- Preliminary seizures with regard to the fight - these are the seizures that provide a convenient starting point for subsequent basic seizures and the conduct of thrusts with them.

CHAPTER FOURTEEN

The Thrusts Method

Thrusts are the methods by which the enemy is thrown from the position of fight costing to the position of fight lying.

Broschi essentially by the feet

In these kind of thrusts, the [sambista's] feet behave against the enemy's feet or body, playing a critical role in the thrust. Thrusts in which actions by foot predate the seizure of the enemy's leg still are considered to be foot thrusts. Broschi's feet have the same steps, hooks, hewings, [podsady], and [podbivy].

• Such thrusts are called steps, with which it [sambist] substitutes foot from behind, front, or outside (from the side) the enemy's foot or feet, and it falls over itself through it with the aid of the jerk by the hands. At the time of the step, both feet [sambista] are concerned with the carpet. Steps are classified as front, back, or lateral.

● By hooks are such thrusts, with which it [sambist] by foot as it seizes one of the enemy's feet and then throws it, [vynosya] hooked foot from under the center of gravity the adversary and by hands deriving it body after the area support.

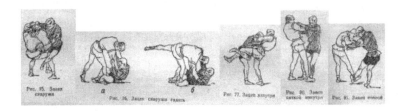

Рис. 75. Зацеп снаружи

а   б

Рис. 76. Зацеп снаружи гадкъ   Рис. 77. Зацеп изнутри   Рис. 80. Зацеп пяткой изнутри   Рис. 81. Зацеп сеносой

Hooks are carried out by the shin, the heel (Achilles tendon), and the back part of the foot. The hook by the shin and by the foot one, and by that foot after one foot the enemy is called by [obvivom]. Concurrent the hook by the foot one foot after the popliteal bend, the second - after it is Achilles tendon other foot the enemy they are named

99

dual by the hook Hooks and [obviy] can be performed as in the counter, so [s] by drop.

• [Podbivami] refers to them as thrusts, and they line the enemy's leg by shin or thigh of [sambista] concomitantly with the jerk by hands with in opposite direction of [podbivu].

It is called a thrust by pickup, with which they line the enemy's leg by thigh or shin from the front, side, or within. The thrust is called [otkhvatom] if the back of the shin lines up with the popliteal bend of the enemy. After lining - this thrust, with which the front of the shin lines the enemy's popliteal bend. The special place it takes up dual after lining, which is done concurrently by two feet in opposite directions. This thrust is known as "by scissors" in folklore.

Рис. 85. Подхват голенью

Рис. 91. Отхват с захватом кости изнутри

Рис. 92. Подбив

Рис. 93. «Подсечки»

• They are called thrusts by hewings, with which, by basic action, causing the enemy to drop, it appears [podbivanie] foot, shin, or the elbow the enemy finger partly sole. Hewings are classified as front, back, lateral, and internal hewings. Because they can be done as in the counter, so [s] by drop.

- They are called thrusts by [podsadami], in which it [sambist] raises the foot or body of the enemy with its foot and turns it over in the appropriate direction with the aid of the hands. They are classified as [podsady] by thigh, [podsady] by shin, [podsady] by lift, and [podsady] by sole.

[Podsady] in the body by the sole or by the shin, with which the enemy is thrust forward through the head throwing, they are known as thrusts through the head. [Podsady] by the shin and thigh can be generated as in the counter, so [s] by drop.

Broschi through the head, [podsad] body [s] by the seizure of two heels, and [podsad] by the lift from within, they are only   carried   out   [s]   by   drop.

Broschi's essence is determined by the body.

These are the thrusts that it [sambist] uses to toss up the enemy's feet or body and move him through itself.

Broschi are classified as thrusts through the pelvic belt, thrusts through the shoulder girdle, thrusts through the back, and thrusts through the breast. Thrusts through the pelvic belt are known as "by Broschi," while thrusts through the thigh are known as "by mills."

• Such thrusts are referred to as thigh thrusts, with which it [sambist] lines up the upper part of the enemy's feet with its pelvic by belt and makes the jerk with its hands in the opposite direction. Broschi through the thigh can be made as an in to counter, as can the drop.

- ""By mills" they are named such thrusts, in which it [sambist] rolls the enemy's body through its arms, resulting in such diverse seizures. Broschi "mill" they can be done as in the counter, so [s] by drop.

• Such thrusts are referred to as thrusts through the back, with which it [sambist] rolls through its opponent's body to spin it.

Thrust through the back, thrust with the seizure hand, thrust with the hearth arm, and thrust with the hearth arm are all conducted out by moving only [s] by drop. The thrust with the seizure hand on the arm, the thrust with the pulling, and the thrust with the seizure hand on the arm are all carried out as in the counter, as is the drop.

• Such thrusts are those with which it [sambist] lines the stomach of the enemy by the lower part of its stomach or two by the hands it tends to help mount upward it breast and stomach and throws it to the right or to the left through its breast. Broschi are only carried out [s] by drop through the breast.

Broschi is essentially defined by his hands.

These are thrusts in which the [sambista's] feet do not concern the enemy's feet or body, and his body doesn't really fall over itself the body of [sambista]; however, in some instances it can be used as an additional fulcrum for the enemy's revolution by back to the carpet. In essence, the enemy rises, is turned over, and is thrown to the carpet by the force of [sambista's] hands.

•Broschi by jerk after sleeve - these are thrusts that it [sambist] derives from equilibrium as well as throws on carpet strong by jerk after sleeve after already being located on the distant the enemy. In the tradition, these are did refer to as removals from equilibrium.

• Broschi by jerk after the foot consists of thrusts, with which one hand seizes foot, A the second - sleeve, belt, forearm under the arm, or it presses on seized foot. Not the foot, not the body [sambista], and they have no direct influence on the feet and the body enemy. Broschi by jerk after the foot include jerk thrusts for the heel, jerk thrusts for the shin, and jerk thrusts for the thigh.

• By thrusts by jerk after two feet, with which it [sambist] seizes both the enemy's feet - immediately or alternately. They are generated without direct action by the feet against the enemy's feet. They join the thrusts by the seizure by two feet, the thrusts [raznokhvatom] by two feet, and the thrusts reverse by two feet in them.

• Such thrusts are called somersault thrusts, and they are achieved by jerking two hands [s] by pressure on the enemy's head or blade. In this case, the foot of [sambista] has nothing to do with feet or the enemy's body. Broschi by somersault they are made up of thrusts by somersault forward and in side.

• Such thrusts are called by revolutions, with which it [sambist] raises the enemy and turns over by hands in air for the thrust to the back. The revolutions of the foot [sambista] do not concern the feet, nor the enemy of the body. In some cases, it [sambist] uses the body as an additional fulcrum for lightening the enemy's revolution. They are divided into three types of revolutions: frontal, lateral, and rearal.

CHAPTER FIFTEEN

Fight Strategy Lying

They introduce two concepts into fight lying technology:

- initial position and auxiliary action.
- Defensive seizures make a breakthrough.
- Stacking up.
- Revolutions are taking place.
- Retention is important.
- Methods that are painful.
- Combinations of the methods combat lying.
- Protection against methods of combating lying.
- Reciprocal methods of combating lying.

The techniques of separating the coupled or captured hands of the enemy are referred to as defensive seizure breakthroughs. They make painful methods or retention in these kind of situations possible, with which you do not have breakthroughs, and it [sambist] would know how to conduct no method.

By stacking up the methods of transferring the enemy from the position known as costing on the elbow or even on the elbows to the situation lying on the spin. They are auxiliary methods that are used to train the enemy in order to conduct retention and painful methods on it.

The methods are called revolutions because they use [nakhodyashegosya] on all fours or lying prone adversary to turn over to the position lying on the spin. They are auxiliary methods that are used to train the enemy in order to conduct retention as well as painful methods on it.

Such actions are referred to as retention when it [sambist] uses its body to force the enemy's body by back against carpet and, without the use of painful methods, retains him in this position for the necessary time.

Methods that are painful

Painful methods - these are seizures, with the help of which it [sambist] exerts influence on the joints of the enemy's arms or legs, putting him in the blind alley.

Methods that cause pain in the hand joints

[Peregibanie] elbow joint The elbow is the traditional name for the lever.

• Outside, unscrewing hand. These methods are known as units because of their interlacing extremities.

• Unscrewing the hand inward. The units refer to such unscrewing as reverse.

Рис. 368. Обратный узел захватом руки между ног

• Jamming biceps.

• Lever arm.

• Painful brush methods are only found in the combat division SAMBO (unarmed self-defense).

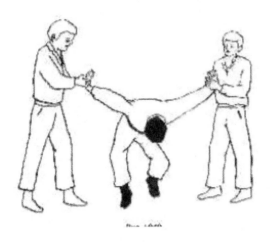

Foot joints are subjected to painful methods.

• By jamming, it is referred to as pressing the tendons of the enemy between the large tibial bone and the beam or large tibial bone [sambista]. They differentiate between the jamming Achilles tendon as well as the jamming flounder-shaped (gastrocnemius) muscle.

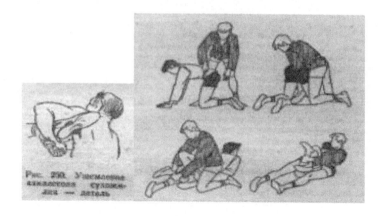

- Knee joint [Peregibanie] The elbow is the traditional name for the lever.

- Methods that cause pain in the hip joints.

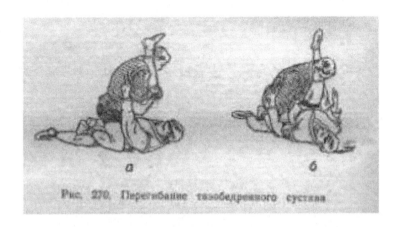

Рис. 270. Перегибание тазобедренного сустава

Passages ranging from the cost of the fight to the cost of the fight lying

• The thrusts and methods of fighting lying are combined.

Рис. 294   Рис. 295   Рис. 296

- Painful   methods,   ready   at   the   counter.

- Transfers to the fight lying as well as reciprocal the fight lying methods against thrusts and enemy coverings.

Passages from of the fight lying to the cost of the fight

- Rising up.

- The combination of getting up and thrusts was mixed.

- Broschi, ready to fight from a prone position.

CHAPTER SIXTEEN

SAMBO Combat (Unarmed Self-Defense)

Combat methods are elements of SAMBO (unarmed self-defense) that have been supplemented with new means and components. This is where dangerous seizures, thrusts, impacts, actions on vulnerable points of the human body, methods of using improvised means, and T.p. come into play.

• Hands make an impact. Hands provide protection from impacts.

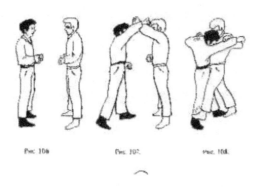

Рис. 106.   Рис. 107.   Рис. 108.

- Footfalls have an impact. Feet provide impact protection.

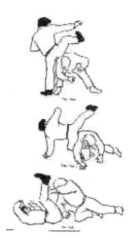

- Seizures that suffocate. Strangling seizures are prevented.

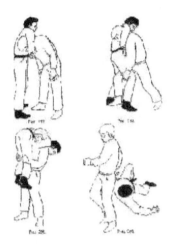

- Protection against seizures and grasps.

- Knives make an impact. Knife protection against blows.

- Impacts with a stick Sticks provide impact protection.

- Impacts are field-engineered by blade. By using a blade, the field-engineer can protect himself from impacts.

• Impacts from a pistol. Protection against pistol attacks.

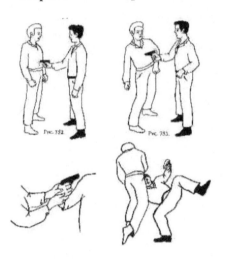

- Bayonet the battle: defense and attack

- Protection from heavy object impacts.

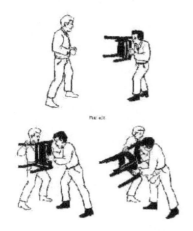

- Make use of the apprentices' resources.

Рис. 809

- Make use of your surroundings.

Рис. 913.

- Mutual benefit and gain

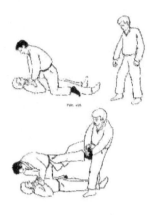

- Safety from the attack is provided by lying.

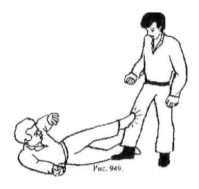

- Protection from multiple attackers.

•Tactics for a group battle,

- as well as detention and tracking

Рис. 913.

- Delayed Inspection

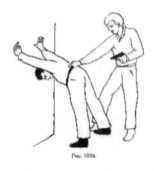

Рис. 1056.

- Binding.

- SAMBO (unarmed self-defense) combat methods are unique (removal of hour; compression and pressure; dangerous thrusts; displacement and the break the vertebrate post).

CHAPTER SEVENTEEN

Playing Environment – Sambo

The match is played on a combat mat ranging in size from 11x11 meters to 14x14 meters. The mat is made from synthetic fabric and also has a smooth surface with a 5 cm or less thickness.

The central surface of the mat, where the bouts are held and which is also considered the main working area, is a 6 to 9-meter-diameter circle. The remainder of the mat, with such a width of 2 to 5 meters, is considered a protective area.

The platform on which the mat is placed must be 2 to 5 meters wider on all sides than the mat. The mat's entire surface is covered with a coverlet produced of firm soft fabric or even some synthetic material with smooth seams.

The covering must always be stretched and tightly fastened. The authenticity and stability of the mat are determined by the chief official, doctor, as well as legislators of the organization hosting the competition.

CHAPTER EIGHTEEN

Equipment – Sambo

Sambo equipment is very similar to that used in mixed martial arts.

Players wear a variety of protective equipment, such as helmets, gloves, and guards. During a fight, the sambovka and belts are worn as part of the uniform. The following are some of the items:

Sambovka

It is a jacket or kimono-style material designed for sambo training and competitions at all levels. Typically, a player will wear a red or blue sambovka with matching shorts and belts.

Sambovka   Helmet   Gum Sheild   Groin Guards   Gloves

Protective Guards

Different types of protective equipment are used by players to avoid injuries or accidents, and these equipment protects the players from the opponent's fatal and dangerous strikes. The following are some examples of commonly used protective guards:

• **Boxing Helmets** – These are all mostly padded helmets worn by boxing or wrestling contestants to protect their heads from injury, cuts, scrapes, as well as swelling. Open-faced helmets with soft or hard plastic ear covers as well as straps all around chin and back of the head are common.

• **Gum Shield** – A mouth guard worn inside the mouth by players to protect their mouth, gums, lips, and teeth from injury.

• **Groin Guards** – These are more like an undergarment worn by players to protect their groins from injury. They are most commonly used in different formats of wrestling or in sports that require vigorous physical activity.

• **Sambo Gloves** – The gloves are padded globes that fighters wear on their hands to protect their hands during a fight. These are designed to injure opponents as little as possible.

CHAPTER NINETEEN

How to Play Sambo

Sambo invented both freestyle wrestling as well as martial arts, as well as its methods as well as wrestling styles are geared toward self-defense rather than attack. It took many years for Viktor Spiridonov as well as Vasili Oshchepkov to perfect the basics of this martial art, and many iconic pioneers of the sport have conceptualized, managed to improve, and perfected the sport since their departure.

In this sport, two players compete in the ring at first, with points awarded for effective grappling or locks. Players start grappling and putting different holds on each other until the game is over. The player is not allowed to strike the opponent down in most sambo styles.

The winner is determined by agile movements as well as different locking skills rather than fast body work. If a player quits during the submission locks while playing, the player is declared the winner. Or else, the winner is determined by the number of points a player has at the end of the match. The rules section explains the rules for the period of the holds and locks, as well as how to declare a winner.

Sambo's Fundamental Strategies

Sambo was originally created as a basic martial art for enhancing hand-to-hand combat. Different formats of art have evolved over time. Generally, the basic style followed in all forms of sambo is a combination of wrestling and

Judo. Players put in a lot of effort to improve their leg lock and ground control skills. In the case of striking, the opponents employ various grappling techniques, the majority of which involve takedowns and submissions.

In most cases of Russian sambo, the primary emphasis is on finishing the game as rapidly as feasible. There are numerous sub-disciplines of sambo, but only five have gained international recognition: Sport Sambo, Combat Sambo, Self-defence Sambo, Freestyle Sambo, as well as Special Sambo. Sport sambo, combat sambo, and freestyle sambo are among those recognized by FIAS.

Sambo Combat

Combat sambo is the most aggressive form of wrestling among all sambo formats, involving multiple kinds of striking as well as grappling. It was created to help people prepare for and survive any type of situation. It was primarily developed and used for military training, and it allows for a variety of aggressive techniques such as punches, kicks, elbows, knees, headbutts, and groin strikes. Combat sambo is used in the Russian military as a training sport for close combat and self-defense.

It incorporates techniques both from sport and self-defense sambo, but employs them in different ways. Combat sambo allows for the use of many techniques that are dangerous and illegal in other wrestling sports. The techniques of this sambo format are very similar to those of modern mixed martial arts. Combat sambo players wear jackets comparable to sport sambo players. Players also wear additional hand protection, as well as shin and head protection on occasion.

Sambo Sport

Sambo is a sport that entails a lot of flinging, ground work, and submissions. This sambo format shares many similarities with Olympic Freestyle Wrestling or Judo, but the main differences are in uniforms, rules, and protocols. For instance, unlike Judo, sport sambo permits some leg locks but not chokeholds. However, in comparison to Judo, there are far fewer restrictions on grips and holds.

Sambo Freestyle

The American Sambo Association created and added freestyle sambo to the sport in 2004. This format of the sport differs from others in that it allows choke holds and other submissions such as certain neck cranks and twisting foot locks. There is no strike allowed in this game, so players must rely on their throwing skills and quick groundwork.

Sambo for Self-Defense

This sport format is primarily used to prepare individuals for self-defense against any armed or unarmed forces. Self-defense sambo is similar to Aikijujutsu. This is primarily intended to train individuals such as bank employees and women in self-defense.

CHAPTER TWENTY

Sambo – Ground Rules

In some instances, the player is declared victorious.

• In the case of a total throw, which can also be defined as a throw in which the attacker does not fall down but the defensive player falls on his/her back or rapidly rolls over his/her back.

• In the case of a painful hold, the opponent gives up or indicates a submission signal by applauding twice on the mat or saying yes loudly.

• In the event of a player scoring more than 12 points more than his or her opponent, the player is declared the winner.

• In the event that the opponent is eliminated from the fight

• Technical explanations and cautions

Technical Outcomes

If a match is tied, the player with the most points for technical actions is declared the winner. Similarly, to avoid ties in a bout, the player with the most activities will be declared the winner. When both players have the same number of evaluation points, the player with the most evaluated holds during in the bouts wins.

Each of these holds has specific points that add to the player's total points at the end of the bout. Similarly, if both players have scored zero points at the end of the match, the winner is determined by the number of activities performed during the match.

According to the Warnings

If both players possess zero technical points or the same number of warnings, the player with the most recent warning evaluation against his/her opponent is declared the winner.

Elimination

A player is eliminated or disqualified from the bout if he or she violates or disobeys the following rules:

• If a player makes a second attempt at a prohibited hold.

• If a player uses more than the two minutes allotted for medical intervention. In this case, the player has been deemed medically unfit to proceed the match.

• Based on a doctor's recommendation, if the player has an inevitable disease or injury.

• If the player receives a third warning during the match, the 3 officials present at the ring will decide.

• If the player does not take a step onto the playing surface within 5 minutes of the first call.

• If a player exhibits rude or inappropriate practices toward his or her opponent or against any of officials or match referees, or if he or she refuses to shake hands with his or her opponent, the player will be disqualified.

Holds That Are Prohibited

Definite holds and actions are strictly forbidden in sambo, and the player who employs them may be disqualified. The following are some of these grips:

• Using a painful grip, throw the opponent on the head.

• Using strangling holds, squeezing the opponent's mouth and nose, and interfering with his/her breathing process.

• Intentionally cause any painful scratches or bites.

• Applying holds to the opponent's fingers and toes.

• Applying painful holds to your opponent's spine or squeezing his or her head with your arms or legs

• To place one's arms, legs, or hands on an opponent's face.

• Use painful holds while standing.

• Apply holds with a jerk. Use the heel portion of your opponent's foot to apply holds.

CHAPTER TWENTY-ONE

Is Sambo Good For Self-Defense?

Sambo is among the best self-defense martial arts to learn. It is one of the few fighting systems which will teach you how and where to fight in any situation. Unlike some other martial arts, Sambo is multifaceted, covering all aspects of fighting, much like MMA. Here are some of the most important skills you will gain knowledge in Sambo that you will be able to apply in street fighting:

• Judo throws as well as sweeps that are extremely powerful
• Wrestling takedowns

• A variety of chokes and joint locks

Strong grappling skills and the ability to take someone down give you a significant benefit in street fighting. Everyone can throw a punch, but not everyone knows how to defend against takedowns or fight on the ground. Carrying the attacker down offers the option of fleeing or establishing a dominant position from which to apply submissions.

Combat Sambo training also tries to teach you how to do damage with punches, kicks, elbows, and knees. This form includes "dirty" techniques such as groin strikes that can be used for self-defense. There aren't many other fighting systems that will teach you how to use illegal tactics or defend against them.

CHAPTER TWENTY-TWO

Distinctions Between Sambo and Many others

What Is The Distinction Between Sambo And MMA?

On paper, Sambo and MMA may appear similar. However, they differ greatly in terms of rules, the manner in which fighters compete, and the uniforms they wear.

Sambo fights take place on wrestling mats, whereas MMA fights take place in a steel cage or a boxing ring.

Sport Sambo fighters are required to wear a red or blue cotton jacket, wrestlers shorts, and shoes. MMA fighters, on the other hand, only wear shorts and just a pair of 4-oz gloves.

Matches in sambo last five minutes. This is much less than in MMA, where matches last three rounds of five minutes each, or five rounds of 55 minutes if a title is on the line.

Because fighters do not have to conserve energy for later rounds, the action in Sambo is extremely fast. MMA moves at a slower pace because fighters must be more proactive in nature and give their all to avoid exhaustion.

Combat sambo fighters, like MMA fighters, can fight both standing as well as on the ground. However, unless they score a knockdown, they do not receive any points for landing strikes. Grappling as well as top control are emphasized. Fighters score the most points when they score a takedown, control their opponent on the ground, or attack through submission. This is not the case in MMA, where judges score both striking and grappling equally.

Despite the fact that these two fighting styles vary in many ways, Sambo is frequently regarded as an excellent foundation for MMA. Sambo fighters in MMA are a difficult matchup for anyone because they are all-around fighters who can fight in any situation. They are capable of striking on the feet as well as grappling on the mats.

What Is the Distinction Between Sambo and Judo?

Sambo evolved from Judo, and the two arts share many similarities. However, Sambo incorporates techniques from those other fighting styles such as wrestling and jujutsu. In addition, unlike judo, Sambo fighters could use strikes to inflict damage, whereas judo is solely based on grappling.

Sambo fighters employ many Judo throws and joint locks, but not all. Sport Sambo fighters are not permitted to use chokeholds, whereas Combat Sambo fighters are. Both forms also permit leg locks, which Judo forbids.

Furthermore, fighters do not solely rely on judo methods to score takedowns. No, they also learn various Greco Roman and capture wrestling takedowns that they would not learn in Judo. When compared to Judo, it's safe to say Sambo is a more well-rounded martial art.

What Is The Distinction Between Sambo And BJJ?

BJJ is a grappling-based martial art that does not use any striking techniques. The goal is to use throws to knock your opponent to the ground so you can offer up them with chokes as well as joint locks.

Sambo, on the other hand, is derived from Judo and comes in two varieties. The first is Combat Sambo, which combines striking and grappling martial arts into a single fighting style. The second is Sport Sambo, which is similar to BJJ in that it is a grappling art that does not include any striking.

Let's compare Sport Sambo to BJJ for the sake of argument:

Fighters compete in BJJ gi by wearing a gi jacket, pants, and belts round the their waist. Sambo fighters all wear the same cotton jacket, wrestling shorts, as well as shoes.

BJJ is all about gaining a dominant position over your opponent and then submitting them. Sambo fighters are not permitted to pull guard, and the action is much more rapid. Sambo focuses on scoring strong takedowns as well as establishing top control.

BJJ fighters are permitted to use chokeholds that are not permitted in Sport Sambo.

BJJ matches last between 2 and 10 minutes, depending on the skill of the fighters, whereas Sambo matches last 5 minutes.

CHAPTER TWENTY-THREE

Champions – Sambo

The International Union of Amateur Sambo (Fédération Internationale de Sambo) is in control of worldwide publicity and sambo events as the sport's international governing body. In 1993, FIAS was split into two organizations: FIAS East as well as FIAS West. While FIAS East encourages the development of sambo in Russian territories, FIAS West encourages the development of sambo in the United States and Other western European countries.

The following are some of the massive world Sambo events accepted or organized by FIAS:

- World Sambo Championships
- FIAS World Combat Sambo Championships
- Russian Armed Forces Championships
- Sambo World Cup
- World Combat Games

Now we'll talk about certain champions who've already made a name for themselves in this sport.

Fedor Vladimirovich Emelianenko

Fedor Vladimirovich Emelianenko is a Russian heavyweight mixed martial artist (MMA), sambist, as well as judoka from the Ukrainian SSR. Throughout his career, he has received numerous awards and accolades in various forms of wrestling, including the FIAS World Combat Sambo Championship (Heavyweight Champion 2002, 2005, 2007).

In 2012, he was incorporated into the FIAS Hall of Fame. In 1998, he also won a gold medal at the Russian Armed Forces Championships. In addition, he served as a brand ambassador for the SportAccord World Combat Games in 2010 and 2013.

Vitaly Viktorovich Minakov

Vitaly Viktorovich Minakov is a Russian sambist, judoka, and undefeated mixed martial artist from the Russian Soviet Socialist Republic.

In the Russian Sambo Championships in 2008, 2009, 2010, 2011, and 2013, he won four gold medals and one silver.

He also won the World Sambo Championship in 2008, 2009, 2010, and 2011. He has also won the Russian Presidential Cup Sambo three times, in 2008, 2009, and 2010.

Igor Yakimov

Igor Yakimov is a judoka and sambist from Russia. He is regarded as one of the most successful sambo champions, having won the World Combat Sambo Championship in 2001. He won the Pan American Sambo Championship in 1998 and 1999. He also won the Russian National Sambo Championship in 1985 and 1988.

In addition to these victories, he was named International Sambo Champion in 1990.

Rosen Dimitrov

Rosen Dimitrov is a sambist expert from Sofia, Bulgaria. He won two gold medals in the World Sambo Championships in 2007 as well as 2011, and also two silver medals in 2008 and 2010.

He as well won the European Sambo Championships in 2008.

He as well as his twin brother Rumen Dimitrov founded the TWINS MMA organization, and they are currently working to develop more talent for it. He has won 21 matches in his career, five by knockout, thirteen by submission, as well as three by decision.

Alexander Vladimirovich Emelianenko

Alexander Vladimirovich Emelianenko is a Russian MMA fighter and sambist who was born in the Russian Soviet Socialist Republic. Fedor Vladimirovich Emelianenko, a sambo legend, is his younger brother.

He did win three gold medals there at Sambo World Championships in 2003, 2004, and 2006. In addition, he won five gold medals and one silver medal at the Russian Sambo Championships in 2003, 2004, 2006, 2010, as well as 2012. In addition, in 1999, he won gold at the European Championships.

Khabib Abdulmanapovich Nurmagomedov

Khabib Abdulmanapovich Nurmagomedov is a Russian SFSR mixed martial artist and sambist. He has did win the Combat Sambo World Championship event twice.

He also competed inside and won the Russian Combat Sambo National Championship. He also is an MMA fighter, and he presently has one of the sport's longest undefeated streaks, with 23 straight wins, eight by knockout, seven by submitting, and eight by decision.

Andrei Valeryevich Arlovski

Andrei Valeryevich Arlovski is a sambist and expert mixed martial artist from the Byelorussian SSR. He won the European Youth Sambo Championship at the age of 19. He also came in second place in the Sambo World Cup. He also won a bronze medal at the World Sambo Championship. He is now concentrating on his MMA career and competing in the Ultimate Fighting Championship.

Printed in Great Britain
by Amazon

86111667R00098